10-22-01

Written by David F. Marx

Illustrated by Cindy Revell

Children's Press®
A Division of Scholastic Inc.
New York • Toronto • London • Auckland • Sydney
Mexico City • New Delhi • Hong Kong
Danbury, Connecticut

For Tabitha, Allan, Amanda, and Connal
—C.R.

Reading Consultants
Linda Cornwell
Coordinator of School Quality and Professional Improvement
(Indiana State Teachers Association)

Katharine A. Kane
Education Consultant
(Retired, San Diego County Office of Education
and San Diego State University)

Library of Congress Cataloging-in-Publication Data
Marx, David F.
    See the city / written by David F. Marx ; illustrated by Cindy Revell.
      p. cm. – (Rookie reader)
    Summary: A boy and his family enjoy the sights of New York City, from cement
sidewalks and ice-skaters in the park to sparkling lights and dancing on a stage.
    ISBN 0-516-22254-6 (lib. bdg.)   0-516-25966-0 (pbk.)
    [1. New York (N.Y.)—Fiction. 2. City and town life—Fiction.] I. Revell, Cindy, ill.
II. Title. III. Series.
PZ7.M36822 Se 2001
[E]—dc21   00-048501

GROLIER
PUBLISHING
1 2 3 4 5 6 7 8 9 10 R 10 09 08 07 06 05 04 03 02 01

Cement sidewalks.

See the city.

Ice-skating in the park.

See the city.

See the city.

13

Sparkling lights.

15

See the city.

Dancing on a stage.

See the city.

So long, city!

Ships on the sea.

9